the HOUR of the
UNEXPECTED

theHOUR

of the UNEXPECTED

by John Shea

ARGUS COMMUNICATIONS
A Division of DLM, Inc.
Allen, Texas 75002 U.S.A.

*Illustrations and cover design
by Mark McMahon*

FIRST EDITION

© **Copyright Argus Communications 1977.**
All rights reserved. No portion of this book may be
reproduced, stored in a retrieval system, or transmitted in
any form by any means—electronic, mechanical,
photocopying, recording or otherwise—without prior
permission of the copyright owner.

Printed in the United States of America.
ARGUS COMMUNICATIONS
One DLM Park
Allen, Texas 75002

International Standard Book Number 0-913592-85-4
Library of Congress Number 77-73648
    5 6 7 8 9 0

CONTENTS

to the Prayer
that always rises
when my family and friends
gather

The Word That Is There

First something happens.

A friend dies; a child smiles us into wonder; an old lady refuses to be old; an adolescent finds a way out; a secret weakness is painfully exposed; we are unexpectedly kissed.

First something happens.

A short fall is suddenly without bottom; an expectation is reversed; a comforting self-image is shaken.

First something happens.

At the center of our best effort we discover our worst motive. Our perfect plot fails and their sloppiest plan succeeds. In single-minded pursuit of one goal we blithely achieve the opposite. When all retreat at the sight of the dead, we stay and stare and do not know why. First something happens.

In these moments, and many more, we are thrown back on ourselves. More precisely, we are thrown back into the Mystery we share with one another. These moments trigger an awareness of a More, a Presence, an Encompassing, a Whole within which we come and go. This awareness of an inescapable relatedness to Mystery does not wait for a polite introduction. It bursts unbidden upon our ordinary routine, demands total attention, and insists we dialogue. At these times we may scream or laugh or dance or cry or sing or fall silent. But whatever our response, it is raw prayer, the returning human impulse to the touch of God.

This is how it was for Jesus. The Kingdom of God which he preached came as a gift, suddenly overtaking the weariness of the soul. In farming a barren field a treasure is stumbled upon; a corner is turned and the perfect pearl is for sale; out of nowhere an invitation to the King's party arrives. The advent of God, even when we are looking for it, is always surprise and any encounter with Jesus always holds the unexpected. To the lawyer who wished justification Jesus gave challenge. The rich young man wanted advice and received an unwanted suggestion.

9

Zacchaeus merely hoped for a glimpse of a prophet yet dined with his savior. The woman at the well came for casual conversation and went away with self-revelation. With Jesus people seldom got what they asked for. They always got more. We pray out of more, when our emptiness is suddenly brimming, when our ravaged lives are called to greatness, when we crash into limits and recoil.

We pray out of our experiences and the Christian Scriptures. We place our personal stories within the Spirit-created story of Jesus. In this placing, in the interaction of the two stories, the deepest meanings of our lives unfold. We discover ourselves in dialogue with the events generated by Jesus, with the personalities who preceded him in faith (Abraham, Moses, Jeremiah) and those who drew faith directly from him (Peter, Mary, Paul). Like all who encounter the Christian story we are spun around. Old worlds are subverted: new worlds rise from the ruins. We are touched by Love beyond love, aware of life within Life. We are timid people suddenly filled with daring. Every word is prayer.

And so the prayers of this book are stories and images, portraits of the human person entrapped and liberated, frightened and thrilled. They record shattering revelations, uncontrolled hopes, fierce desperations, moments of dance and tears. In all this they resonate with the crazy farmers, persistent widows, cheating accountants, wily servants, forgiving fathers, and uninvited guests of Jesus' parables. They remember the courage of Mary, the betrayal of Peter, the abandonment of Magdalene, the fidelity of God, and the compassion of Christ. At times these prayers directly address God; at other times they do not. Yet all are witnesses to grace, stuttering accounts of the God whose ways are not our ways.

In the end there is only one justification for these prayers. When God either muscles or smuggles his way into our activities, we know all words are betrayals; yet we speak. At that moment prayer is neither guilt nor task but just the word that is there.

A PRAYER TO JESUS

If you drank with the IRS of your day
and traded laughs with whores
yet took time with the bravado of the young man
and knew the wealth of the widow's mite

If you knew
that each man's righteous vision
is built from the splinters of his brother's eye

If you knew
that only earth and human spit
can cure blindness

If you knew
that sun and rain are without prejudice
and wind blows where it will

If you knew
the fresh flesh of lepers
soon forgets its birth

If you knew
why sepulchers are painted white
and the chalices of filth polished

If you knew
that some men sweat blood
while others sleep

then you know

I am both thieves
scrounging for the kingdom
and cursing the cross.

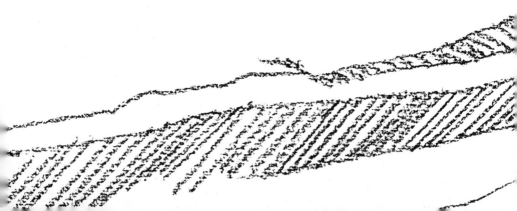

A PRAYER FOR YOUNG MEN IN AN OLD WORLD

Yesterday
you told me
the clouds carried a New Age.
All was malleable to the tender request,
kisses transformed twisted lips,
flowers grew through snow.

Now
prophecy no longer tears the air,
flames no longer dance
on your young heads.
Time has robbed you of breath
and in the spaces of your panting
whispered its weary wisdom:
dreams are foolishness,
the heart a lie.

Now
the hurt and angry questions
are in your eyes.
"Why did not the tearless city descend to earth
when we held hands on the boulevard of song?
Why did not the fist open and the bomb bay close
when we played naked in the meadows and the lakes?
Are we left with a chemical Eden
or a patch of monastery to make too much of
or the deadening prospect of
a raise after three months
and the sad memory of youth:
I once saw Christ on a white horse?"

Slumped men,
gibbeted on the intractable heart,
parched by vinegar kisses—
beware surprise.
It is the hour of the unexpected.

A PRAYER OF TAKING STOCK

Lord,
this winter night
I have sharpened myself
like a bookkeeper's pencil
bent over random entries.

This winter night
there will be no balance.
The fragments of memory
will not be pieced into a story.
The days are so themselves
they will not gather into weeks.
Each moment is alien to every other,
a life of blazing fireworks,
beautiful and gone,
extinguished in the black and trackless sky.

This winter night
truth will have its way.
I will remain cluttered
like my desk—
beneath a book I've never read
a year-old phone number
of someone I've forgotten.
It will remain a runaway life
with the reins beyond reach
and the rider's eyes blasted into amazement
by the winds of tomorrow.

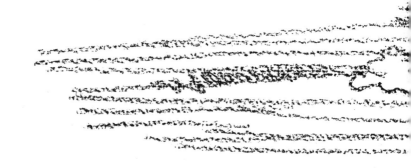

THE LAST PRAYER OF PETITION EVER
(written between New York and Chicago 35,000 feet up)

Sigmund Freud has put me wise
that God is merely the me
afraid to face the exploding crash of a 747
from the inside.

Also it is common knowledge
that doctors reserve the back wards
for people who daddy God for daily bread.
Of course theologians, always the last to know,
keep asking for little red wagons
while everyone else is buying them at Sears.

So
heaven is not stormed by my "gimmes."
I no longer beg God
"to make mine enemies
the footstool under my feet."
I am busy with the upholstering myself.
My prayer life has taken a collegial,
adult, Vatican IIish turn.
I do not beseech a mercy or beg an intercession
(needless to say importuning is out)
but consult with the Senior Partner
on affairs personal, social, and cosmic.

So it is
I wonder who was addressed
when in the sudden drop of an air pocket
my heart relocated to the space behind my teeth
and someone sitting in my seat screamed,
"O my God don't let the plane fall!"

A PRAYER FOR TENDERNESS

The stone throwers gather for judgment
in the immaculate, white-walled office
of the parish rectory.
Their target grips the chair,
her fingernails blanch.

She is young enough
to crack gum and giggle;
old enough
to turn her voice to ice,
her eyes to flint.

Just yesterday
a rabbit died from her blood
proving beyond doubt
she is no longer alone
inside her skin.

For once in her life
she wishes
she was alone.

Her father, who by his own admission
is no fool, does not understand.
Her mother wants to know
how she could do this to her.
Her date who scored
is home doing algebra
but his father assures all
the privilege of the car
will not be Jim's for a long time to come,
a very long time to come.
The priest scribbles
in the sand.

It is now too much.
Her innocence breaks
and spills down her face.
The righteous
whose virtue cannot comfort
have no chalice
to gather those tears.

She stops, straightens.
In search of tenderness
she moves within herself
in primitive descent
to that warm, wet place
where clings her hated child.

A PRAYER AT THE BARBER SHOP

It was a magazine to wait by,
nothing more,
page leafing, picture looking, backgrounding
the mindless talk of the barber shop.
It fell open on my lap
and the exploding nakedness of a young girl
raced down a napalm road toward me.
I tried to look away
but her nightmare eyes held me.
In her screaming mouth was my name.
I wanted to move on to Salem streams
or Marlboro Country or even a Buick
To Believe In but like the hobos in Godot
I said let's go and did not move.
I watched her burn.

The next page was a year later.
She had been healed.
All the skin of Viet Nam
had grafted her back to beauty.
She wore a white first communion dress
with a blue bow at the waist
and that reticent smile
which is Oriental forwardness.

That photo of a restored yellow girl
with her out-of-sight skin surgically pinched
is the never-ending apology of man to his neighbor.
We kiss and make better
what first we wound and make worse.
But thank God for that resurrection picture.
It keeps me from the growing fear.
If she is carnage,
my most tender moment is cruel,
my achieved world the camouflage of death.

A PRAYER FOR THE LADY WHO FORGAVE US

There is
a long-suffering lady
with thin hands
who stands on the corner
of Delphia and Lawrence
and forgives you.

"You are forgiven,"
she smiles.

The neighborhood is embarrassed.
It is sure
it has done nothing wrong
yet everyday
in a small voice
it is forgiven.

On the way to the Jewel Food Store
housewives pass her
with hard looks
then whisper
in the cereal section.

Stan Dumke asked her
right out
what she was up to
and
she forgave him.

A group
who care about the neighborhood
agree that if she was old
it would be harmless
or if she was religious
it would be understandable
but as it is . . .
They asked her to move on.

Like all things
with eternal purposes
she stayed.
And she
was informed
upon.

On a most unforgiving day
of snow and slush
while she was reconciling
a reluctant passerby
the State People,
whose business is sanity,
persuaded her into a car.

She is gone.
We are reduced
to forgetting.

A PRAYER OF LOST PURPOSE

He slept after dinner now.
In his favorite chair
with his belt loosened.
The paper slid from his lap.
He dozed fitfully for he was afraid
Norman Rockwell would sneak into the den
and paint him.
He would enter Americana
in his marshmallow middle years
stuffed with affluent steak
and toasty with radial heat.
And oh god how he longed after
a cold depression corner
where men stamped their feet
and blasted the night with their breath,
their fists clenched against tomorrow.

THE PRAYER OF THE OLDER BROTHER

I dreamed
they never saw me—
but then they never did—
my sweated eyes only a moment lifted
from the stubborn land
to catch the blur of foolish father
his robes clutched up,
rivers washing down his beard,
his sandals lost in run
falling on the runaway,
the inheritance thief,
sniffling back to sonship
the music of welcome in his ears
the fatted calf of forgiveness in his teeth.

I woke
the way rejection wakes,
bypassed and bitter.
The only comfort—
no comfort at all—
there are no older brothers.

A PRAYER TO THE SLEEPLESS GOD

Better a sleepy god
who dozes while men plot
or a god of graft
paid off in prayers
than this insomniac,
pacing the night sky,
missions smoking in his mind,
two star-blazed eyes raking the earth
where his worshippers wait,
not knights of glory
but broken men
who have found the source of healing.

THE PRAYER OF THE COMMUTER

The latest incarnation
of God is stalled
outside the city walls.
He has been betrayed
into a traffic jam
by the kiss of the urban planner.
He is the reluctantly still point
in a 55 mile-a-hour world.
The expressway,
having had its way with him,
hands him over
to the crucified intersection
where the light
is eternally red.
He is nailed in the left-turn lane.

At home,
behind locked doors,
his wife worries the pot roast
to overdone.
His children wait
amid cold lima beans.
Suddenly
the rushing wind
of a car in the driveway.
The thunderous slam of a door.
And lo!
By divine button the garage door
has been rolled away and the Son of Man
appears on a cloud of exhaust.
He is as a stranger
and moves past his wife and children
without a word.
He reaches into the refrigerator
and their hearts burn within them
as they recognize him
in the drinking of the beer.

A PRAYER OF ANGER

No hymn of praise today.
No hand-clapping alleluia
for the All-Good God
and his marvellous handiwork.
Lord,
a child has been born bad.
He gangles and twitches and shames
the undiscovered galaxies of your creation.
Why could not the hands that strung the stars
dip into that womb to bless and heal?
Please no voice from Job's Whirlwind
saying how dare I.
I dare.
Yet I know no answer comes
save that tears dry up, skin knits,
and humans love broken things.
But to You who are always making pacts
You have my word on this—
on the final day of fire
after You have stripped me
(if there is breath left)
I will subpoena You to the stand
in the court of human pain.

THE PRAYER OF BELIEF: A LITURGICAL CREED

We believe that where people are gathered together in love
    God is present
    and good things happen
    and life is full.

We believe that we are immersed in mystery
    that our lives are more than they seem
    that we belong to each other
    and to a universe of great creative energies
    whose source and destiny is God.

We believe that God is after us
    that he is calling to us
    from the depth of human life.

We believe that God has risked himself
    and become man in Jesus.

In and with Jesus we believe that each of us
is situated in the love of God
and the pattern of our life
will be the pattern of Jesus—
through death to resurrection.

We believe that the Spirit of Peace
is present with us, the Church,
as we gather to celebrate
our common existence,
the resurrection of Jesus,
and the fidelity of God.

And most deeply we believe that in our struggle to love
we incarnate God in the world.
And so aware of mystery and wonder,
caught in friendship and laughter
we become speechless before the joy in our hearts
and celebrate the sacredness of life
in the Eucharist.

A PRAYER FOR SACRED THINGS, SACRED NO LONGER

The sacred pearl
on the forehead of the goddess
has fallen to mere wealth.
The impenetrable mystery of white light
is bitten, priced, and strung
around blasphemous necks.

The Tree at the Center of the Earth
under which Buddha sat
and on which Jesus hung
has been cut into real wood beams
for the ceiling of the games room.

The many mansions in the Kingdom of the Sky
have been leveled
for the highway of interstellar traffic.

Even man,
once immortal jockey
soul rider of the body,
is now dispensable coefficient,
producer, consumer, casualty.

We are the keepers of the garden
but must our mastery turn everything opaque?
Can nothing be more than it is?
Are we left
with the eucharistic world
ground down to bread
and the horrible boredom of a wine
which refuses its mission of blood?

A MEMORIAL PRAYER

His fingers were sausages about to burst
that skittered over the endless tweed of his vest.
His tie-knot was hidden under folds of neck
which terraced to a cavernous mouth and stockade teeth.
His nose battled for breath and his eyes
were permanently sewn open with delight.
Covering the rest of Jonathan
was a cape and propping it up a cane.
Ted Klasser called him
the fattest fop in history.

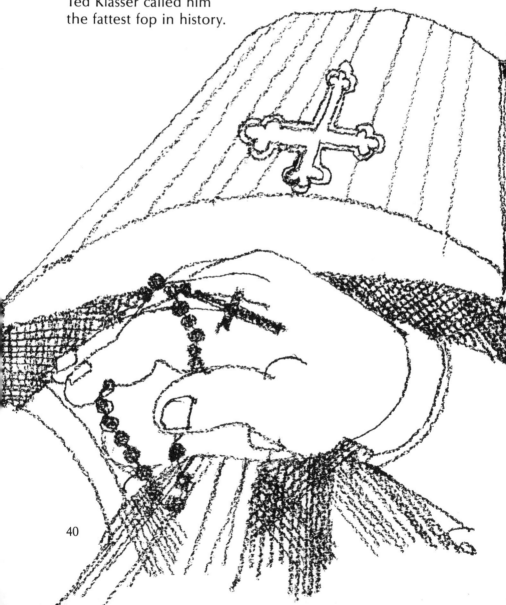

On one beer Jonathan traveled to a sun-burnt
Pacific atoll where weight was divinity
and he ruled anemic natives as a god.
On two beers his trunk,
formerly disguised as an arm,
flailed the air, sucked the table for peanuts,
scarfed up a third beer, curled it inward to his mouth,
pachyderm style, and with its downing
a serious Jonathan talked of love.
He wasn't fussy.
Anybody with different but compatible equipment.
"Why can't fat boys and fat girls get together
and compare bulges?"

On the bright beach days of summer
Jonathan would retreat to the "Comfortably Cool" Clark,
remove the arm rest on the outside seat in the tenth row,
and talk to the movie screen.
Once while warning the Panama-suited Sidney Greenstreet
of Humphrey Bogart's nefarious intentions
he was ushered to the sidewalk.
He vandalized the billboard.
"The Clark theatre is unfair to Sidney Greenstreet
and lookalikes."

Death is worthy of tears and torn hair.
Jonathan's was a pratfall and a banana peel.
A heart attack did not claim him
as his doctor had promised.
He choked on a chicken bone.
At the funeral Ted Klasser said that
everytime he left something on his plate
he would think of Jonathan.
It wasn't a god damn eternal flame
but it was some sort of a memorial.

THE PRAYER OF MARIANNE WISNESKI

The Kingdom of God is like Marianne Wisneski
who is thirty-two years old
and who always hides her left hand
because as her mother said,
"The only gold you'll ever have
will be in your teeth."
To make things worse
every day for lunch
she has rye crisps and a diet Pepsi.
And lately she has taken
to crying in the ladies room.

Yesterday
she was graced
by a more-than-ordinary brushing against
in the elevator.
Albert Scynowicz who works in shipping
said excuse me but he had two tickets
to The Who.
That night
to uninterrupted FM
she curled her legs under her on the couch,
allowed her eyes a mist of hope,
and to her surprise
found in her mouth,
like tax money in a fish,
a prayer.

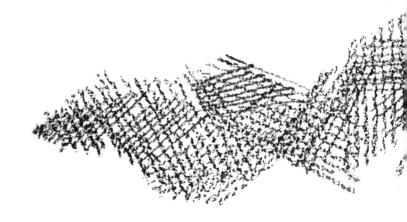

A PRAYER FOR THE SECRET SOLIDARITY
OF THE HUMAN RACE

The man I did not notice
yesterday died today
and left me alone.

A PRAYER TO THE MAD DOLLMAKER

Lord God,
you are too much like us.
When lonely,
you make mistakes.
When love struck,
you are impetuous.

But it was folly
to fall upon the unsuspecting earth,
knead a body of clay
and laying on it,
feet to feet, hands to hands,
breathe passion down its mouth
and wake the eyes to wonder
with tears.
When you put no key in its back
but trusted it to the heat of the heart
and the dimness the mind calls light
we knew, old dollmaker,
that you had gone mad.

Some say
you never guessed
til your love-child came to you
in the beauty of the garden and asked,
"When you die
will all this be mine?"

THE RESURRECTION PRAYERS OF MAGDALENE, PETER, AND TWO YOUTHS

Like her friend
she would curse the barren tree
and glory in the lilies of the field.
She lived in noons and midnites,
in those mounting moments of high dance
when blood is wisdom and flesh love.

But now
before the violated cave
on the third day of her tears
she is a black pool of grief
spent upon the earth.

They have taken her dead Jesus,
unoiled and unkissed,
to where desert flies and worms
more quickly work.

She suffers wounds that will not heal
and enters into the pain of God
where lives the gardener
who once exalted in her perfume,
knew the extravagance of her hair,
and now asks her whom she seeks.

In Peter's dreams
the cock still crowed.
He returned to Galilee
to throw nets into the sea
and watch them sink
like memories into darkness.
He did not curse the sun
that rolled down his back
or the wind that drove
the fish beyond his nets.
He only waited for the morning
when the shore mist would lift
and from his boat he would see him.

Then after naked and impetuous swim
with the sea running from his eyes
he would find a cook
   with holes in his hands
   and stooped over dawn coals
who would offer him the Kingdom of God
for breakfast.

On the road that escapes Jerusalem
and winds along the ridge to Emmaus
two disillusioned youths
dragged home their crucified dream.
They had smelled messiah in the air
and rose to that scarred and ancient hope
only to mourn what might have been.
And now a sudden stranger falls upon their loss
with excited words about mustard seeds
and surprises hidden at the heart of death
and that evil must be kissed upon the lips
and that every scream is redeemed for it echoes
in the ear of God and do you not understand
what died upon the cross was fear.
They protested their right to despair but he said,
"My Father's laughter fills the silence of the tomb."
Because they did not understand they offered him food.
And in the breaking of the bread
they knew the impostor for who he was—
the arsonist of the heart.

After the end
comes the conspiracy
of gardeners, cooks, and strangers.

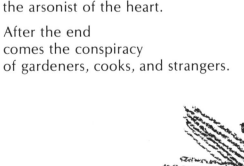

A PRAYER OF DISCIPLESHIP

Trade blood with me, brother and sister, and conspire
to unravel the wrappings of our lives
to gain the consoling terror of truth.

It might be one of those classic dupes
like the Holy Grail or the Fountain of Youth
or a wild charge on some suspicious windmill
beating the air and impersonating truth.

But some things must be done
out of folly or pride or sin
to fly into the sun
to stand against the wind.

You and I
we sniff like bloodhounds through the forest of our lives
to catch a scent of where Meaning paused,
breathless and heaving from our pursuit,
then plunged again into the thicket
where we lost him and our youth.
And in those thickets our middle years will snag
until down a final and forgotten trail
where at last Meaning will be met
he will suddenly turn to greet us
with the bony hand of death.

But, brother, we both dimly see
   the struggle is the goal
   the search is what we know.
All the rest is heaven.

Then
when despair was ripe and bursting
the hand of a laughing angel
pushed me over the edge of Sunday afternoon.
Down the screaming cliffside of my soul
I scraped for a handhold.
The black beach rushed upward.

There
on that black beach
in the everlasting night
I let loose the choking grip I had on life
and the thieving sea swirled round me
and escaped down the sand
with all I ever held in my hand.

Now of a sudden, of a sudden
in this moment of my breaking
came the absurd dawn of hope
and embryonic God began his growth.

So arbitrary, so crazy
like shooting dice for apostleship
or listening for the spirit in the wind.
Like some mythic Greek, astride the stars,
from an ornate urn slung on his shoulder
had poured a terrible beauty
over the earth.

And so, brother, in this runaway comedy
we bungle through
a pilgrim is stretched across the sky
and I will cast my lot with him
   for fellowship and more
he is a man like me
      and more
   who will scream the absence of his God
         and die
      then leave behind some Palestinian knoll
         at dawn
            a broken tomb.

A PRAYER AT BURGER KING

He was accustomed to making women laugh
and saying blushing things
which forced them to stare downward
into cups of coffee they never saw.
So when Alice called the third time
and knowing how hard it is
for heavy girls to get a date,
he suggested lunch at Burger King.
He wore his blue blazer and white turtle neck
which made it clear to all
that Whoppers were not a habit
but the slumming quirk
of a man used to better.
He gave Alice a quick progress report
on his miraculous rise at Zenith.
She was into God
and told him he was empty
at the center.
Jesus could stuff his hollowness
and he could lean on her
in his misery.
After that
he did not answer her letters
and when she phoned
he suddenly discovered guests.
But he spent time at the mirror
wondering
if his winning smile
was really fiercely gnashed teeth
and his hard, clear eyes
the site of future weeping.

A PRAYER OF UNWARRANTED HOPE

Lord,
if I believed that Satan,
as St. Peter says,
roams about seeking whom he may devour;
I would say
he had made a meal of her.
All her words were ugly:
all her thoughts were schemes.
She took revenge
on anyone
with judgment poor enough
to love her.
Her only tears
were icicles of spite
and she slapped away
the hands of help.

Now
she tells me
the demon has moved out.
She is a house swept clean,
a space of pirouetting light.
And I am caught
once again
in the embarrassment of hope
which this time did not have the good manners
to merely glimmer
but the beautiful rudeness
to burst.

A PRAYER TO THE EVER-ENTICING GOD

I am embarrassed for you, God.
A promising paradisiacal beginning
that fizzled, nothing to show
but some murdered messengers
and a crucified son rescued three days
after the nick of time.
And recently you have tripped
into the credibility gap.
You are a joke in academia,
the household pet of rectories,
and everyone is saying you have to be rethought.

And now look at you,
acting out for attention.
A lampshade on your head,
making faces for laughs,
insisting Paul said party always
not pray.
And now you come to me
with a fiddle and a jug
and the grasshopper notion
to entice my ant-like industry,
to strike a tune and dance off with you
into the long winter.
Are you kidding?
Let's go.

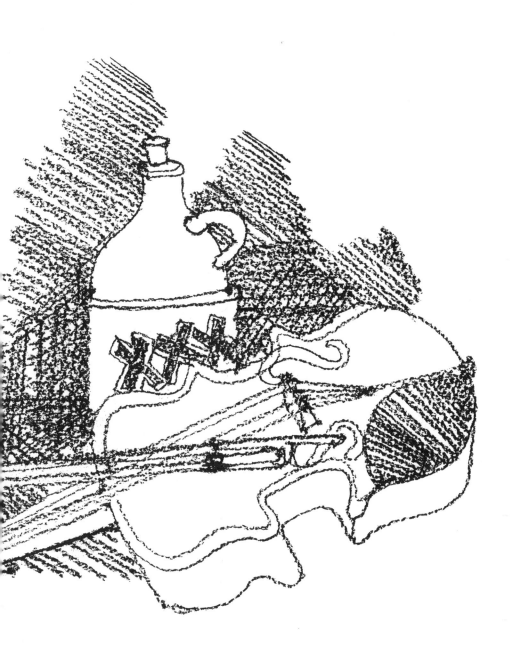

A PRAYER OF DEATH

On retrospect
it was more than an unwitting contraction
and a pelvic push,
more than the spine knitting
and the synapses wiring
in those nine months.
Courage was making a small fist
in the dark warmth.
A glaring passage of light
promised me the world
and I trusted it.

Now
they wait around my bed
with cups of hospital coffee.
The doctor says I've slipped
but I have only clenched the sheet
because an unmoored sun wants to warm me.
The glaring passage of light has returned.

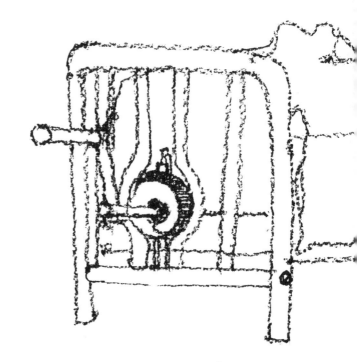

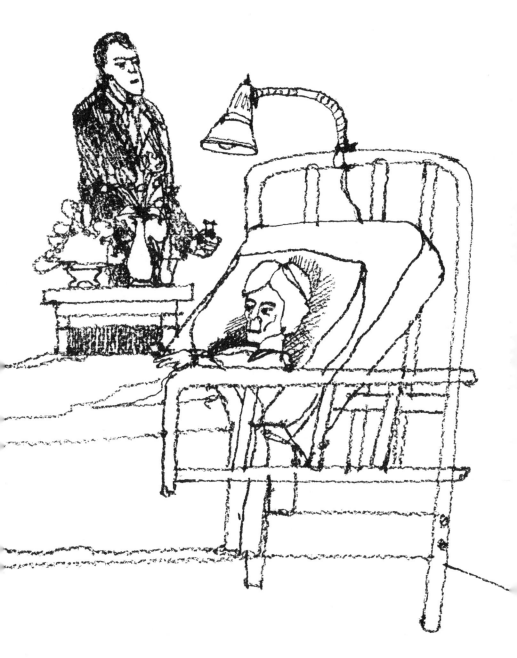

A PRAYER THE WORLD CANNOT TAKE FROM YOU

Like an obedient cat
the purse sat
on her lap.
Her fingers slowly traced
the creases on her forehead.
Her eyes were closed
against the worries
of the waiting room.

Without warning
her lower lip gave way.
A string of dribble
fell to the collar
of her coat.
A sudden handkerchief appeared.
She had old people's ankles.

Out of the inner office
past the smile of the nurse
he stepped
buttoning a gray sweater.
Skin gathered in mounds
on the back of his hands.
He wrestled with a coat
that fit him once.
Her eyes opened. He took her hand.
"Let's go."
"Yes."
and he led her into the dark, December afternoon.

TWO PRAYERS OF LOSS

I.
Thaddeus Edward Bornowski
would not be at the lathe today.
It was the 24th of June
and he was angling his kitchen chair
down the narrow back stairs.
It slid perfectly into the trunk
of his car. It had been there before.

It was seventeen minutes to St. Adelbert's
and three winding, five mile-an-hour minutes
to the Holy Rosary section
and just a moment past
the stone bead of the Annunciation
to Rosemary Dorothy Bornowski
    1909–1968

He set the chair on the side,
leaned over with kitchen intimacy,
and talked downward
past the plaque and grass,
the settled dirt, cement casement,
and the copper casket with the crucified God
to the listening memory within.

II.
For Daniel and Mary O'Malley
after supper came the beads.
He would Hail Mary the first part:
she would Holy Mary him back
   and the rote prayer rose to chant,
   word ran upon word, a marriage sound,
   the Catholic trick for ecstasy.
Every evening for forty-seven years.

Now she was gone.
The family agreed their father
had held up well
but every night after supper
in the den of his daughter's house
he would Hail Mary
and wait.

THE PRAYER OF SOMEONE WHO HAS BEEN THERE BEFORE

After the last time—
  when I finally turned from flight
  and from somewhere came the strength
    to go back—
I rummaged the ruins,
    a refugee picking through bombed belongings
    for what surely was destroyed
and began again.
  I grew my new life
      thick and rough
    with an alarm system on the heart
    and an escape hatch in the head.
It was as spontaneous
as a military campaign.
  I loved in small amounts
    like a sick man sipping whiskey.
Each day was lived within its limits.
Each moment swallowed quickly.
    It was not all—our embracement of life
      but neither was it the hunched
        and jabbing stance of the boxer.
There was courtesy and a sort-of caring.
  It was not bad.

Now this.
This thing   This feeling
  this unbidden intrusion
    which had no part to play
  but played it anyway.

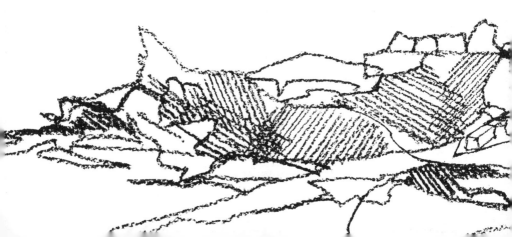

All those things scrupulously screened out
want in.
   And I can sense it coming,
     a second coming,
      a second shattering.
   Someone   Something
     is at me once more,
  mocking my defenses,
   wrenching my soul.
     God damn it!
Is it you again, Lord?

A PRAYER FOR AN OLD LADY EVER YOUNG

"Peace to all who dwell in this house."
The priest stamps snow on the hall rug.
"And a good morning to you, Mrs. Kurleen."
Hannah is pillowed round,
wedged into uprightness,
before the morning game shows.
A dark red lipstick is almost on her lips
and the beauty parlor has recently
strategically deployed her thinning hair.
"Hello, young man."
Click. Magic waves
knock the telly into unconsciousness.
"I want to go to confession first."
She winked
promising more
than ordinary fare
and launched in.
"I had some impure thoughts
    but I suppose you never had any of those—
        being a priest."
"Only when I'm around you, Hannah."
"I yelled at my daughter ten times."
"Only ten."
    She hits the priest on the shoulder
    and laughs.
"You don't get any good sins when you're old."
"For your penance
tell your daughter
you are a crotchety old lady."
"No."
"Tell her you are sorry for being bitchy."
"No."
"Blame it on your arthritis."
"Alright."
Hannah smooths her lap
and wheedles.

"Is it true about Mrs. Mallory's daughter Meg?"
"How would I know?"
   "Ah! I see it is."

"I hear the Altar & Rosary . . ."
but a round, white Jesus,
rescuer of priests,
rises before her eyes,
slips between her lips,
and manages
by the sheer breadness of him
to stop the conversation.
Water eases the host down
and Hannah leaves
wet, smeared, red lip prints
on the glass.
Suddenly she is old.

The priest packs up.
"Merry Christmas, Hannah."
"Merry Christmas, Father."

The snow of his entrance
is now a dark, wet slash.
It will soon disappear
into the rug.

"Hannah,
your hair-do
is so wickedly attractive
that it's a proximate occasion of sin."

"Thank you, young man,"
she laughs and buttons
the T.V. back to life.

SHARON'S CHRISTMAS PRAYER

She was five,
sure of the facts,
and recited them
with slow solemnity,
convinced every word
was revelation.
She said
they were so poor
they had only peanut butter and jelly sandwiches
to eat
and they went a long way from home
without getting lost. The lady rode
a donkey, the man walked, and the baby
was inside the lady.
They had to stay in a stable
with an ox and an ass (hee-hee)
but the Three Rich Men found them
because a star lited the roof.
Shepherds came and you could
pet the sheep but not feed them.
Then the baby was borned.
And do you know who he was?
Her quarter eyes inflated
to silver dollars.
The baby was God.
And she jumped in the air,
whirled round, dove into the sofa,
and buried her head under the cushion
which is the only proper response
to the Good News of the Incarnation.

PRAYER AT GENESARETH—MARK 5, 1-20

Holed up within me,
his eyes bleeding
   in the crouched darkness,
is a frightened, cellar creature,
the stunted, mongoloid me.

He lurks in guarded depths.
My fear is vigilant.
By day
   I overtalk his cries
and if at night he howls
      I shut my soul
         and play at sleep.

Then Jesus
   pushed off course
   by a meddlesome squall
crashed on my shore.
With the first syllable
of his unwanted words
like a sudden pregnancy

he stirs.
Even prayer and fasting
are now helpless against
the force of his
delivery.

He rips.
Bolts.
Out the mouth of my screams
down the cheeks of my tears.
In the nakedness of his exorcism
his deranged features betray
the practiced sanity of his keeper.

There is no hospitable pig
for easy habitation
or a death-dealing cliff
to bring him rest.
The poor bastard is loose
and he is mine.

I will search him out
among the pliable words of pity
and the delighted face of shock.
I will fall on him with kisses,
swallow him down,
and await our redemption.

A PRAYER TO THE GOD WHO WILL NOT GO AWAY

Lord,
you are the poetry of wordless lives,
the salting of tasteless purposes,
the reminder that we are more than
the sinking spiral of the dying sparrow
and that the reckless rush of the galaxies
marvel at the human collision of a kiss.
You are the tightening hope
that someone has stretched a net
beneath this high wire act of ours.

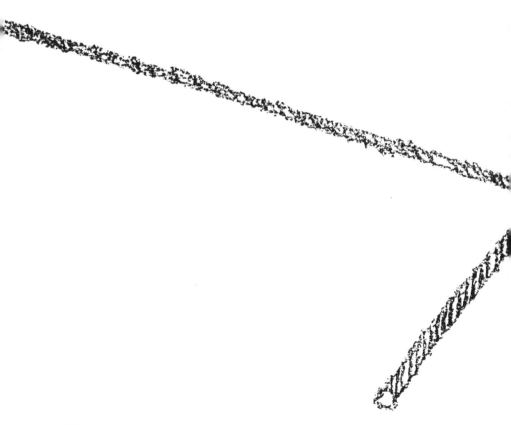

AN EASTER PRAYER

Lord of Easter,
the words of death . . .
nodule . . . malignant . . . mastitised
are boiled killingly clean,
passed on by forceps.
None of the slop of life is on them.
They do not well up and spill over
or sadly sparkle or break
into syllables of laughter.
They are under orders
to dispatch without recourse.
Begging will not move
these unyielding words of stone
which only you roll back,
Lord of Easter.

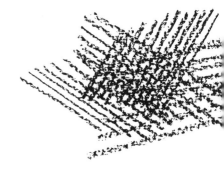

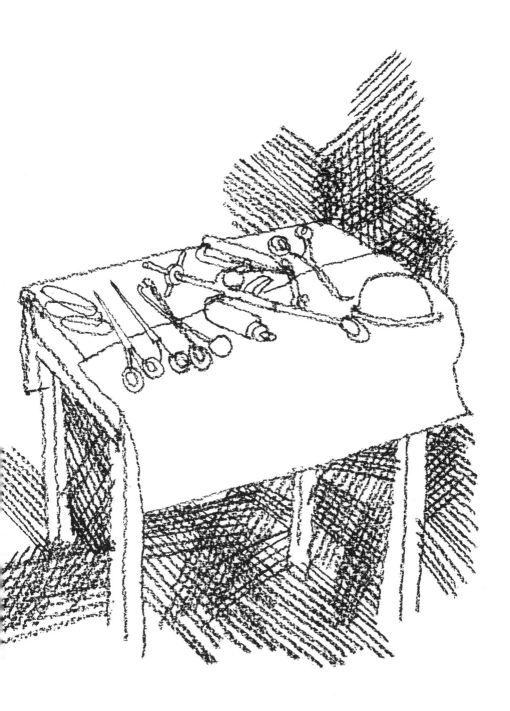

THE PRAYER OF THE HOLY SACRIFICE OF THE MASS

Those who do not believe in a Higher Harmony
will balk when told an accident crunched
in the parking lot at the very moment
the altar boy's nose began to bleed.
He bled on the surplice, the cassock,
the candle, the other altar boy,
and the priest's unlaced shoe
which bulgingly carried an Ace bandaged ankle.
The priest was stuffing a purificator up the boy's nose,
damning the blood into his eyeballs,
when the lector asked "how do you pronounce
E-l-i-s-h-a?" and the organist pounded
the entrance "Praise to the Lord."

They processed.
The bleeding, the halt, and the mute
unto the altar of God.

Saturday was late and liquored
and delivered God's people,
sunglassed and slumping, to the epilogue
of weekend life, the Gothic Church.
They were not the community of liberal theology
nor the scrubbed inhabitants of filmstrips.
They were one endless face
and that face was asleep.

"May the grace of our Lord . . ."

A hungry pause for repentance.
A quick feast of sins.

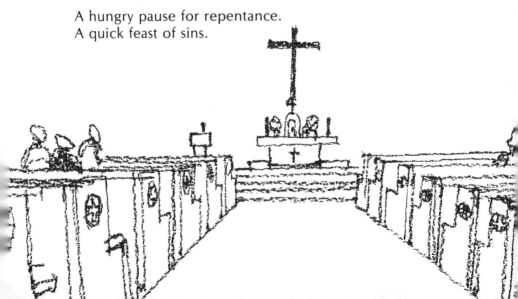

The lector murdered the prophets once again
and bypassed the section where a certain E-l-i-s-h-a
was having prophetic truck with a widow.
The homily parlayed a fairly clear gospel
(you are either with me or against me)
into sentences of vacillation
and paragraphs of double-think.
The priest ran to the Creed for refuge
only to find a special creed was prepared
for this morning's liturgy by Mrs. Zardek
"I believe in butterflies and the breath of . . ."

The courage of the president
of the liturgical assembly
drained into the bolt holes
of communion rail days.

The offertory gifts never made it.
They were dropped by an elderly couple
("We never liked the new Mass anyway.")
who collided with a small but speedy child
whose highheeled mother was in klicky-klack pursuit
and whose name was "Rodgercomeback."

The consecration was consistent.
The priest lifted the host
and said "This is my blood."
Instantly aware of his eucharistic goof
but also momentarily in the grip of a bizarre logic
he changed the wine into Jesus' body.
Then
with his whole mind, heart, and soul
he genuflected
        —never to rise—
to a mystery which masks itself
as mistake
and a power which perfects itself
in weakness.

THE ADVENT PRAYER

What will come
when all the days
have run upon the nights
and all men climb the tree of Zaccheus
and stretch necks beyond giraffes
to be the first to be blazed
by a star?

We are badly in need of ecstasy.
We freeze in sun and fever in shadows.
We die
amid the flowers of the mind.

Someone
must come to us from the future
prodigally
with rings and robes and kisses
and fall upon our self-reproach
with the tears of welcome.

The star-child is turning
in the womb of the virgin.
We dwell in readiness.
Override the babble of our words
with the raw cries of new life.

Be born, stubborn child.
We wait.

A PRAYER FOR NEW MUSIC

Jesus said
we play dirges and do not mourn,
frantic rock and do not freak out.
A new music must be heard
which will drive us to dance
in a world wrung into flatness.
Tonight will we not all sleep
   with one ear in dream
and one alert
   for the crackling of concrete
   and the blossoming of earth?

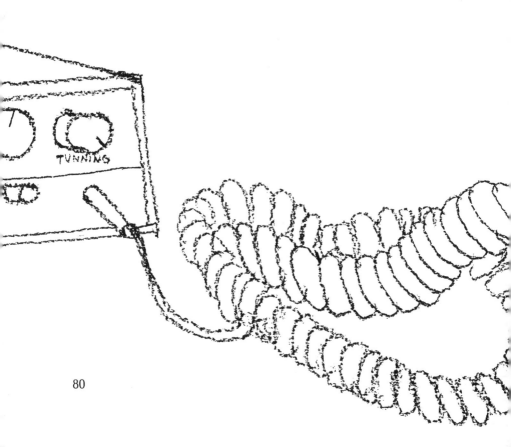

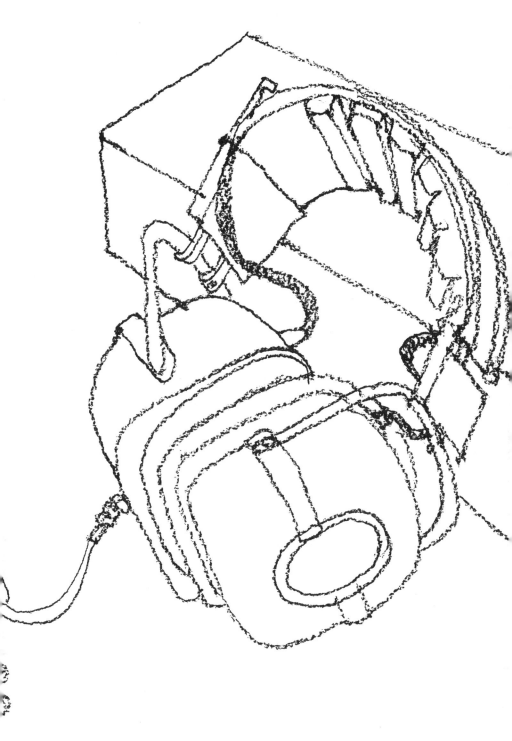

A PRAYER TO THE GOD WHO WARMS OLD BONES

Locked arm in arm,
the wool of winter still around them,
three old women hobble
across the young grass of June.
They have staged a geriatric escape
from St. Andrew's Old People's Home
but varicose veins have forced them
to rest on the bench outside my window.
They settle down for an afternoon
of people watching.
No one can resist.
The boy with the baseball mitt says hi.
The truck driver waves. The mailman
asks how the girls are today.
They giggle and think him silly.
The ladies on the bench believe life
is friendly and when it is not,
they scold it
like a child who must be told he is good.
Yet they wait
(and so do we)
for a passerby, an afternoon visitor,
perhaps that woman
with the baby in the stroller
to tell them the good news—
they do not need coats in summer.

A PRIESTLY PRAYER ST. JOHN WOULD NOT APPROVE OF

As usual
I come beaten—
a romantic who knows better
but cannot stop,
a wound down dervish,
his schemes done in by grace,
his glorious quest after the brightest star of winter
ending in a very bad cold.

My priesthood has not lacked causes.
I have marched for peace, picketed for grapes,
sensitized my psyche at Bethel,
gave up sure-fire advice for the Rogerian mirror
(from which now leers the militant Carkhuff)
but I cannot run off to hula hoop salvation,
"putting on Christ" with my Jesus sweatshirt.
I know the exact time of the Second Coming
can only be told on a Mickey Mouse watch.

Ghosts of priests past rise up:
some sons of Eli, the temple gang,
others struggling prismatics refracting
the unapproachable light of God
onto the technicolor earth.
They bequeath both bread and stones,
fishes and serpents.
Yet gifts are gifts.
They gamble—not without regret—
and wonder if people who look back
really turn to salt.
And in the fidelity of their doubt
they call me back,
   their brother in a foreign land,
to my pact of blood with You.

I must return to the Listening Place
to be healed beyond forgetting,
to celebrate without ego tripping,
to find a meaning which is not the best told lie.
I must remember the scatological faith
that You once sneaked off to the woods with the world
and we are the slow gestation of Christ.
In You the most tired truth will be fresh
and I will surrender to victory and find a peace
which is the limitless source of fight.

A PRAYER OF AMENDMENT

The purgatorial sauna runs last night's bourbon
to the boards and the ditty which inspired
the dawn cab home moans over electric rocks.
Stretched on the hot slates of regret
a modest towel protects the rights
of private perspiration.
The dry heat works a chemical metanoia
on the soggy soul and the dissolute fun
of the old man sweats into the constancy of the new.
Under a shower of ice,
an oath of repentance,
a firm purpose of amendment,

and close upon it

like a self-evident truth
or an inalienable right
in the instant of recovery
the profligacy of the imagination
draws another beer.

A PRAYER TO THE GOD BEYOND GOD

Architect, Body-Moulder, Breath-Giver
Mountain-Thunderer, Goatherd,
Sky-Dweller, Dream-Stalker,
Freedom-Fighter, Desert Shiek,
Bridegroom, Wine-Grower, Potter,
Law-Giver, King-Breaker, Jealous Husband
Judge, Ruler, Priest
Father
Flame, Wind, Gentle Voice,
Grave-Robber, Spirit-Giver
Islam knows you
as the joy
that can only go
ah

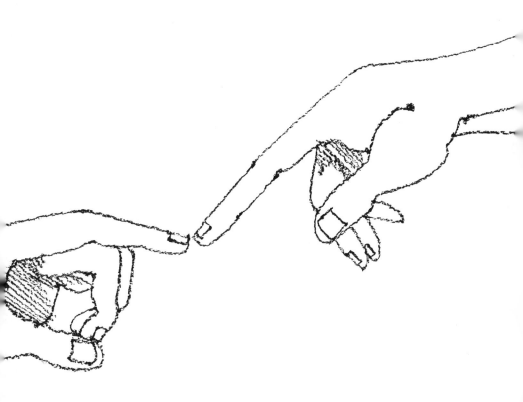

A PRAYER OF WHOLEHEARTED COMMITMENT

Lord,
You have the biblical reputation
of taking people places
they never wanted to go.
Witness Jonah
delivered by whale to Nineveh
and Habakkuk
flown by angel to Babylon.
Also I have heard
You do not consult.
Abraham is suddenly ordered from Haran
and Moses called out of retirement
for the Egypt assignment.
Furthermore
Paul says
You take a chiropodist's delight
in Achilles heels,
spurn eloquence for the stutter,
and reveal yourself
in the thorns of the flesh.
And what was this unpleasantness
with your Son shortly before
his appointment at the Right Hand?
So it is that to You
my most resounding "yes"
is a "maybe"
and it is with one eye on the door
that I say
"Behold, Lord, your servant waiteth!"

A PRAYER OF ABANDONMENT

We know ourselves
by the ghosts we fight
    the apparitions of a sleepless night
whom we blast in rage,
treat to cold steel speeches of resolve,
and confide lusts that will not bear the day.
So where were you last night, my good time deity;
    drinking buddy, frat brother
when failure was in my throat
and every word a scream for peace.

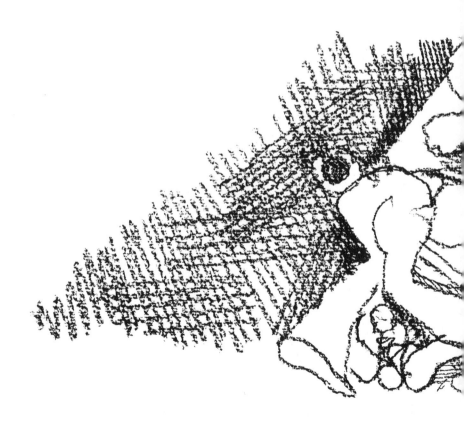

A PRAYER TO THE GOD OF SURPRISES

Attack
when the sun has turned the lake to flame
and the waves are music on the beach.
Ambush me
in the quiet beyond words
I have with her.
Spring at me
from the running boy.
Vanquish me
in the courage of the weak.
Take me by surprise
in the wrinkled smile
of the lady with the floppy hat.
But be warned.
I will be on my guard
welcoming defeat.

A PRAYER TO THE AWESOME GOD

I have seen the kingdom children
ark dancing in the temple,
psalming and cymboling,
coaxing grace with a parade of summersaults,
turning your fierce lightning
into sparklers of joy.
They are the lap sitters, the ear whisperers,
tracing a smile on your lips
with the child's confidence
that your heart is laughter.

Forgive
my bowed and kneeling distance
and my Old Testament stutter
when I remember
that the outspread wings of eagles
cover you
and your face is death.

PRAYER FOR A NUN IN A WHEELCHAIR

In the Convent of Perpetual Adoration
on an eternal summer afternoon
the three o'clock chimes called back
the flight of the old nun.
In her wheelchair
before the God who lives in bread
and runs the risk of staleness
she watched the hour
that Peter, James, and John did not.
Two young ones come for her
with the precise steps of piety
and perpendicular genuflections.
The guard is changed.
She is pushed from the adoration space
but the bright white God goes with her
in the monstrance behind her dimming eyes.
The sacred has performed its slow alchemy.
The wheelchair hypnotically clacks
the revolutions of her exit.
She is maneuvered by the sister on duty
to a sparse clean room with a crucifix and flowers
and placed in the windowed light
where she dwells with silence
and the memory of praise and
the dancing particles of the undying sun.

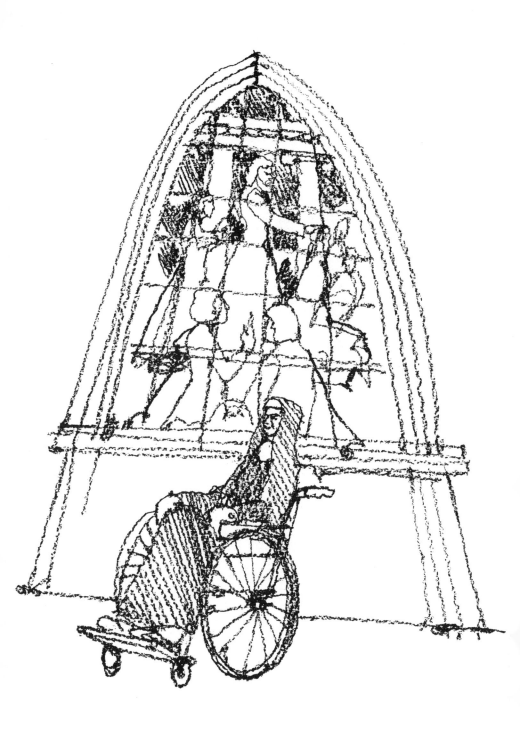

THE LAST PRAYER OF THE MAN WHO CANNOT PRAY

The sun which Ecclesiastes says always rises
streaked across the water, lit the shore
like a stage and forced the lone man
to shade his eyes against the overbearing day.
Shoeless, hatless, slacks rolled knee high,
a limp half-opened shirt, a pale sculpting
the night left upon the beach.
Spent white caps foam about his feet
and slip like desperate handholds
back to sea. Sand grips his toes,
sucks tight his heel, cements his arch.
He eases loose. Two perfect prints.
A wave rushes the beach, spreads and runs
upon the prints, blurring, erasing.
Another comes, washing away, smoothing.

The lone man pushes into the sea.
Darkness swirls about his waist,
splashes his chest. He cuts the water
with strong, sure strokes. His kicks
send up a spray. A majestic wave
towers above him.

A PRAYER TO THE PAIN OF JESUS

Father,
when crutches were thrown away
did your Son limp
after the running cripples?

Did Jesus' eyes dim
when Bartimaeus saw?

Did life ebb in him
when it flowed in Lazarus?

When lepers leapt in new flesh
did scales appear
on the back of his hand?

The gospels say
Jesus felt power go out from him
but neglect to say
whether at that moment
pain came in.

Did the Son of God
take on ungrown legs and dead eyes
in the terrifying knowledge
that pain does not go away,
only moves on?

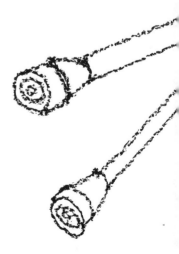

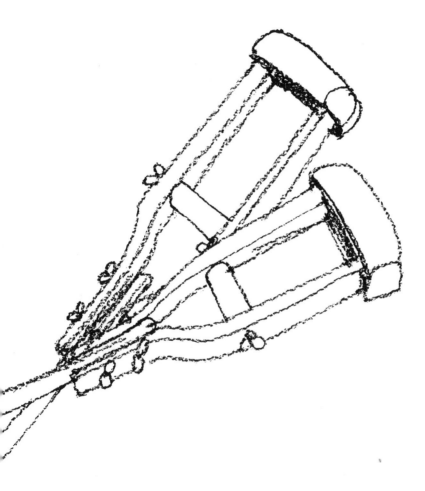

A PRAYER FOR THE LONG HAUL

Allow me not, Lord of Blood,
to be one with the One
and mountaintop smile
on the trashing plain.
Allow me not, Lord of Bone,
to drive out ambition with a whip of dreams
and smuggle heaven onto the troubled earth.
Allow me not, Lord of Flesh,
escape ecstacy, the inner endless journey,
the noiseless perfections of the soul.
Give me, Broken Lord, the long courage
for compromised truths, small justices,
partial peaces.
Keep my soul in my teeth, hold me in hope,
and teach me to fight
the way farmers with hoes defeat armies
and rolled up manuscripts survive wars.

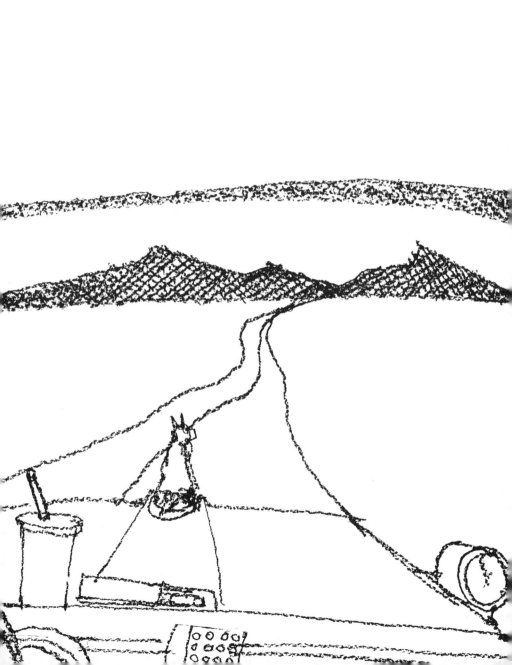

A PRAYER FOR BAPTISM

Lord Jesus,
to the disciples' bewilderment
you said,
"Let the little children come unto me."
And so now we gather
   parents, relatives, friends
in the name of this child
   who cannot yet run to you
and ask
that you come to her.
We suspect that in your Father's plan
babies are sent to disarm us.
Our shields are useless
against their simplicity.
May this child as she grows
in age, wisdom, and grace
ever remain the bringer of your peace,
Lord Jesus.

A PRAYER OF CHRISTMAS PAST

What boy pulled his stocking cap over his ears
(his unmessable crew cut beneath)
and found the predawn Christmas snow
waiting for him?

The street lights were city stars
guiding magi through the supernatural night.
The boy's holy ambition was to walk the snow
without leaving tracks,
to know everything it was
yet leave it unmarked.
He failed wonderfully
across Romaine's white lawn.
Two blocks away
the bright Gothic God
invited him into the magic darkness
where ears were bells
and nose was pine and incense
and eyes were poinsettas and golden chalices.
As was his host's custom
he surprised him,
like a gift under the tree,
and took him up past the stained glass saints
to the vaulted, wood-carved heaven.
He told the boy he would not fall
then dropped him into Christmas.

What man now strikes the flinty past
to fire the coldness of his soul?

A PRAYER TO THE GOD WHO LIVES IN CHILDREN
(for Liam)

Two foot, two year confluence of bone
and love and blood with bathing suit
slung on roguish hips, hair
that blonds the beach, in primitive pact
with air and sea, sent from
All There Is to blandish sated eyes

when was it

in your bowlegged pursuit
to love wrestle the fleeing cat
or when your pinball face
hits jackpot over a soggy chip
chanced upon in the lawn
or in your mercurial, non-nap hours
when drunken, prodigal smiles
are drowned by waterfall eyes

when was it,

predator of weary adults,
with what burst or flash
or the throwaway grace
of a Charlie Chaplin fall
did you become
the sacrament of God?

A PRAYER FOR THE CHURCH

Not alone
the passage through the knives and kisses
but you and me and her
and that one with the running eyes
and the man with the incision in his side
and the lady in the size sixteen petite,
a band which camps around the last of light
and tells the story of the broken Son
about the fusion of all men's wrists
and the single eye of God
and tomorrow's march
toward the breaking greyness of the sky.

THE PRAYER OF ISAAC'S BIRTH

The angel said
the withered shall conceive
and Sarah laughed
at the thought of a geriatric egg
wheelchairing down a fallopian tube
to rendezvous with Abraham's exhausted thrust
wheezing and crutching its way toward
collision
which is the sidesplitting hello
of the bar of soap, the cream pie,
the banana peel, the bombing bird,
all things beyond prediction
which loose logic's hold
on the Laurel and Hardy world.

And now you burst in,
pulling back the drapes of a sunless life,
singing off-key enough to wake the dead.
I had forgotten
that for the friends of the storyteller
the impossible is ever happening.
Confinements crack, the caves of permanence
give up their guests
for from the mouth of the resurrected Christ
comes the laughter of Isaac's birth.

A PRAYER TO MARY AT THE CROSS

On the hill outside the walls
beneath the brutalized memory of New Person
reels the struggled magnification of the Lord.

Woman,
the dead rain falls
and the earth grows cold
and your son no longer
swallows the sky.
But a song of hope
must be struck upon the strings
about fallen sparrows and counted hairs,
the painful prayer of that widow with her mite,
the prophetic fierceness of the sun,
the fire of the desert stars
under which rings the adamantine No of Jesus
to the promises of the Prince
and the everlasting echo in your womb—
Fear not: God stirs.